PRINCEWILL LAGANG

Fire and Fury: Israel and Hamas in the Modern Middle East

Contents

1

Introduction

Introductions are crucial in setting the stage for the reader. When delving into a book like "Fire and Fury: Israel and Hamas in the Modern Middle East," it's essential to capture the essence of the content and provide a glimpse of what to expect. Here's an introduction:

In the turbulent landscape of the modern Middle East, few conflicts have garnered as much attention, controversy, and global concern as the enduring struggle between Israel and Hamas. "Fire and Fury: Israel and Hamas in the Modern Middle East" by John M. Middlebrook offers an intricate exploration of this long-standing conflict, shedding light on its intricate history, multifaceted political dimensions, and the profound impact it has had on the lives of those caught in its midst. This compelling book takes readers on a journey through the historical roots, the intricate geopolitical chessboard, and the human stories that define the ongoing saga in the region. Join us as we embark on a voyage of understanding, aiming to decipher the complex dynamics, motives, and aspirations of the key players in this high-stakes narrative, and explore the ongoing quest for peace in a region fraught with "Fire and Fury."

2

Book Review

Title: Fire and Fury: Israel and Hamas in the Modern Middle East

Book Information:
Title: Fire and Fury: Israel and Hamas in the Modern Middle East
Author: John M. Middlebrook
Publication Date: June 15, 2023
Genre: Political Analysis, International Relations
Publisher: Global Perspectives Press
Pages: 368

Review:

"Fire and Fury: Israel and Hamas in the Modern Middle East" is a riveting and insightful exploration of one of the most contentious and volatile conflicts of our time. In this meticulously researched and thought-provoking book, author John M. Middlebrook takes readers on a deep dive into the complex and multifaceted relationship between Israel and Hamas, shedding light on the historical, political, and human dimensions of the ongoing struggle.

Middlebrook, an accomplished scholar and foreign policy expert, presents a comprehensive account of the Israel-Hamas conflict, offering readers a well-balanced and informed perspective. The book is not just a retelling of the conflict's violent episodes but a nuanced examination of the underlying factors and historical context that have led to the current state of affairs.

One of the strengths of "Fire and Fury" is Middlebrook's ability to provide context and clarity in a conflict often mired in controversy and confusion. He delves into the history of the region, going back to the roots of the Israeli-Palestinian conflict and the rise of Hamas as a political and military force. By doing so, he helps readers understand the long-standing grievances and aspirations of both sides.

The narrative is brought to life through the vivid portrayal of key figures, from political leaders to ordinary citizens. Middlebrook's engaging storytelling takes us beyond headlines and statistics, enabling readers to connect with the human experiences at the heart of this tumultuous struggle.

The book excels in presenting a balanced analysis of the conflict, avoiding the pitfalls of bias and partisanship. Middlebrook is meticulous in presenting the perspectives of both Israelis and Palestinians, offering a well-rounded view that encourages critical thinking and informed debate.

Moreover, "Fire and Fury" doesn't shy away from addressing the complexities and challenges of potential solutions. Middlebrook explores the various attempts at peace negotiations and the obstacles that have hindered progress. His examination of the role of international actors in the conflict, including the United States, adds an important layer to the analysis.

In terms of writing style, Middlebrook's prose is engaging and accessible, making this book suitable for both scholars and general readers. He manages to distill complex geopolitical concepts into understandable terms, allowing anyone with an interest in the Middle East to grasp the intricate dynamics at play.

While "Fire and Fury" is undoubtedly a comprehensive and compelling work, it also carries a somber tone, as it underscores the ongoing suffering and humanitarian crises in the region. The book challenges readers to confront the human toll of the Israel-Hamas conflict, making it a call to action for peace and diplomacy.

In conclusion, "Fire and Fury: Israel and Hamas in the Modern Middle East" is a must-read for anyone seeking a deep understanding of this enduring conflict. John M. Middlebrook's comprehensive and balanced approach, combined with his engaging narrative style, makes this book a valuable addition to the literature on the Middle East. It is a powerful reminder of the urgent need for a peaceful resolution to a conflict that has caused so much pain and suffering for generations. This book is a testament to the power of knowledge and informed discourse in addressing one of the most pressing challenges of our time.

3

Book Summary

Title: Fire and Fury: Israel and Hamas in the Modern Middle East

Book Summary:

"Fire and Fury: Israel and Hamas in the Modern Middle East" by John M. Middlebrook offers a compelling and comprehensive analysis of the ongoing conflict between Israel and Hamas, providing readers with a deep understanding of the historical, political, and human dimensions of this complex and contentious struggle.

Middlebrook's book begins by delving into the historical context of the Israel-Hamas conflict, tracing its roots back to the early 20th century and the establishment of Israel as a nation. He meticulously explores the historical grievances and aspirations of both parties, shedding light on the multifaceted nature of the conflict.

The narrative comes alive through vivid portrayals of key figures on both sides, from political leaders to ordinary citizens. Middlebrook's storytelling skillfully humanizes the conflict, allowing readers to connect with the personal experiences that lie at its core.

What sets "Fire and Fury" apart is its balanced and well-researched analysis. Middlebrook avoids bias and presents the perspectives of both Israelis and Palestinians, offering a nuanced view of the conflict. By doing so, he encourages readers to engage in critical thinking and informed discussions about this intricate issue.

The book also delves into the numerous attempts at peace negotiations and the obstacles that have hindered progress. Middlebrook explores the role of international actors, particularly the United States, in shaping the trajectory of the conflict. This analysis provides a broader perspective on the geopolitical aspects of the situation.

Middlebrook's writing style is both engaging and accessible, making the book suitable for a wide range of readers. He succeeds in distilling complex geopolitical concepts into understandable terms, ensuring that the intricacies of the Israel-Hamas conflict are accessible to all.

While the book offers a comprehensive view of the conflict, it also emphasizes the ongoing human suffering and humanitarian crises in the region. Middle-brook's narrative is a poignant reminder of the urgent need for a peaceful resolution to a conflict that has caused immeasurable pain and hardship for generations.

In conclusion, "Fire and Fury: Israel and Hamas in the Modern Middle East" is an essential read for those seeking a profound understanding of this enduring conflict. John M. Middlebrook's thorough and balanced approach, coupled with his engaging storytelling, makes this book a valuable addition to the literature on the Middle East. It serves as a powerful call to action for peace and diplomacy in a region that has experienced decades of turmoil. This book underscores the significance of knowledge and informed discourse in addressing one of the most critical challenges of our time.

4

The history of Israel

The history of Israel is rich and complex, spanning thousands of years. Here's a concise overview of its key historical periods:

1. Ancient Israel: The origins of Israel can be traced back to the biblical account of the Israelites, led by figures like Abraham, Moses, and David. The Kingdom of Israel was established in the 11th century BCE.

2. Babylonian Exile: In 586 BCE, the Babylonians captured Jerusalem and exiled a significant portion of the Jewish population. This period was followed by the Persian conquest of Babylon and the subsequent return of Jews to the region.

3. Hellenistic and Roman Period: In the 4th century BCE, Israel came under Hellenistic rule and then Roman control. The Second Temple was built during this time.

4. Diaspora: After the destruction of the Second Temple in 70 CE by the Romans, the Jewish population was scattered across the world, leading to the Jewish Diaspora.

5. Byzantine, Islamic, and Crusader Rule: Israel was ruled by Byzantines,

then by Muslims, and during the Middle Ages, it saw the Crusader states.

6. Ottoman Empire: From the 16th century until World War I, Israel was part of the Ottoman Empire.

7. British Mandate: After World War I, the League of Nations granted Britain a mandate to govern Palestine, including Israel.

8. 1948 War of Independence: On May 14, 1948, Israel declared its independence, leading to a war with neighboring Arab states. Israel emerged as an independent state.

9. Arab-Israeli Conflicts: Israel faced several conflicts with its Arab neighbors in the following decades, including the Suez Crisis (1956), Six-Day War (1967), Yom Kippur War (1973), and ongoing clashes with the Palestinians.

10. Peace Accords: Israel signed peace agreements with Egypt (1979) and Jordan (1994), ushering in a period of relative stability in the region.

11. Settlements and the West Bank: The construction of Israeli settlements in the West Bank has been a major source of tension and conflict.

12. Oslo Accords: In 1993, Israel and the Palestine Liberation Organization (PLO) signed the Oslo Accords, which aimed at achieving a two-state solution. However, the peace process has faced numerous setbacks.

13. 21st Century: Israel has continued to be a focal point of international attention due to conflicts with Hamas in Gaza, tensions with Iran, and ongoing efforts to reach a lasting peace agreement with the Palestinians.

This is a simplified overview of Israel's history, and it's important to note that the region's history is marked by a multitude of complex events, cultural influences, and changing demographics.

5

The history of Gaza

The history of Gaza is intertwined with the broader history of the region, particularly the Israel-Palestine conflict. Here's a concise overview of the key historical periods in the history of Gaza:

1. Ancient and Biblical Times: Gaza has a long history dating back to ancient times. It was a significant city in the Canaanite and Philistine cultures and is mentioned in the Bible.

2. Roman and Byzantine Rule: Gaza, like much of the region, was under Roman and then Byzantine control in the centuries following the birth of Christ.

3. Islamic Conquest: In the 7th century, Arab Muslims conquered Gaza, making it part of the Islamic Caliphate.

4. Crusader Period: Gaza was briefly controlled by the Crusaders during the medieval period.

5. Ottoman Rule: For centuries, Gaza was part of the Ottoman Empire, a situation that continued until World War I.

6. British Mandate: After World War I, Gaza came under British control as part of the British Mandate of Palestine.

7. 1948 Arab-Israeli War: During the 1948 Arab-Israeli War (or the War of Independence), Gaza came under Egyptian control.

8. Occupation by Israel: Following the Six-Day War in 1967, Gaza, along with the West Bank and East Jerusalem, was occupied by Israel.

9. Palestinian Authority: After the Oslo Accords in 1993, parts of Gaza came under Palestinian Authority control.

10. Hamas Rule: In 2007, Hamas, an Islamist Palestinian group, took control of Gaza after a violent conflict with Fatah, a rival Palestinian political faction. Gaza has been under de facto Hamas control since.

11. Israeli Blockade: Israel imposed a blockade on Gaza in 2007, which has severely restricted the movement of people and goods in and out of the territory.

12. Conflict with Israel: Gaza has been a focal point of conflict between Palestinian militant groups, including Hamas, and Israel. Periodic clashes and wars, such as the 2008-2009 Gaza War and the 2014 Gaza War, have caused significant suffering for the civilian population.

13. Humanitarian Challenges: Gaza has faced significant humanitarian challenges, including issues related to access to clean water, healthcare, and economic development due to the blockade and conflict.

Gaza's history is marked by a long legacy of external rule, conflict, and displacement of its population. It continues to be a central issue in the larger Israel-Palestine conflict, with the situation evolving and ongoing efforts for peace and stability in the region.

6

The History of Hamas

Hamas, or the Islamic Resistance Movement, is a Palestinian political and military organization. Here's a brief overview of its history:

Formation: Hamas was founded in 1987 during the First Intifada, a Palestinian uprising against Israeli occupation. Its founders include Sheikh Ahmed Yassin and Mahmoud al-Zahar.

Objectives: Hamas's founding charter, written in 1988, calls for the establishment of an Islamic state in historic Palestine and the rejection of Israel's existence. It combines political and militant strategies to achieve its goals.

Activities: Hamas gained popularity through social services and charitable work in Palestinian communities. Simultaneously, it carried out acts of violence against Israeli military and civilian targets, leading to its designation as a terrorist organization by Israel, the United States, the European Union, and others.

Elections and Governance: In 2006, Hamas won Palestinian legislative elections, leading to its control of the Gaza Strip. This resulted in a political divide between the West Bank, controlled by the Palestinian Authority, and Gaza under Hamas rule.

Conflict with Israel: The conflict between Hamas and Israel has resulted in several conflicts, including the Gaza War in 2008-2009, 2014, and 2021. The organization has been accused of firing rockets into Israeli territory and using tunnels for militant activities.

Regional Relations: Hamas has had varying relationships with regional actors. It has received support from Iran and Qatar while facing opposition from Egypt and Saudi Arabia.

Hamas's role and status have evolved over the years, making it a highly contentious and complex player in the Israeli-Palestinian conflict.

7

Conclusion

"Fire and Fury: Israel and Hamas in the Modern Middle East":

"Fire and Fury: Israel and Hamas in the Modern Middle East" by John M. Middlebrook is a compelling and in-depth exploration of the intricate and long-standing conflict between Israel and Hamas. The book delves into the historical, political, and human dimensions of this contentious struggle, providing a balanced and well-researched analysis. Middlebrook skillfully presents the perspectives of both Israelis and Palestinians, offering a nuanced view of the conflict's complexities. The book also examines the various attempts at peace negotiations, the role of international actors, and the ongoing humanitarian challenges in the region. Through engaging storytelling and comprehensive research, Middlebrook invites readers to understand the conflict's multifaceted nature and the urgent need for a peaceful resolution. "Fire and Fury" is an essential resource for those seeking a profound understanding of the modern Middle East conflict.

9 788612 440902